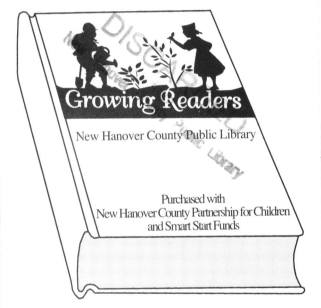

George Washington

by Barbara Knox

Consulting Editor: Gail Saunders-Smith, Ph.D.

Consultant: Mary V. Thompson, Research Specialist
Mount Vernon Ladies' Association
Mount Vernon, Virginia

Pebble Books
an imprint of Capstone Press
Mankato, Minnesota

Pebble Books are published by Capstone Press
151 Good Counsel Drive, P.O. Box 669, Mankato, Minnesota 56002
http://www.capstone-press.com

1 2 3 4 5 6 08 07 06 05 04 03

Library of Congress Cataloging-in-Publication Data
Knox, Barbara.
    George Washington / by Barbara Knox.
    v. cm.—(First biographies)
    Includes bibliographical references (p. 23) and index.
    Contents: Early life—The Revolutionary War—The first president—Life after
the presidency.
    ISBN 0-7368-2082-5 (hardcover)
    1. Washington, George, 1732–1799—Juvenile literature. 2. Presidents—United
States—Biography—Juvenile literature. [1. Washington, George, 1732–1799. 2.
Presidents.] I. Title. II. First biographies (Mankato, Minn.)
E312.66 .K58 2004
973.4'1'092—dc21   2002155681

Note to Parents and Teachers

The First Biographies series supports national history standards for
units on people and culture. This book describes and illustrates the
life of George Washington. The photographs support early readers
in understanding the text. This book also introduces early readers to
subject-specific vocabulary words, which are defined in the Words
to Know section. Early readers may need assistance to read some
words and to use the Table of Contents, Words to Know, Read
More, Internet Sites, and Index/Word List sections of the book.

Table of Contents

Time Line

1732
born

George Washington was born in Virginia in 1732. He grew up on a farm. George went to school for a short time. He mostly studied at home.

People can see only the outline of the house where George was born.

a map George drew in 1748

Time Line

1732
born

1748
begins to work
as a surveyor

George began to work as
a surveyor when he was 16.
He measured land in Virginia.
He made many maps.

George (left) surveyed land in Virginia.

Time Line

1732
born

1748
begins to work
as a surveyor

1759
marries
Martha Custis

In 1759, George married Martha Custis. She and her two children came to live at George's plantation. It was called Mount Vernon.

◄ George and Martha (center) were married in 1759.

Time Line

1732
born

1748
begins to work
as a surveyor

1759
marries
Martha Custis

1775–1783
leads army in
Revolutionary W

The Revolutionary War began in 1775. George led the army of American colonists. They fought against Great Britain. The war was long and hard.

George (on white horse) led soldiers in many battles.

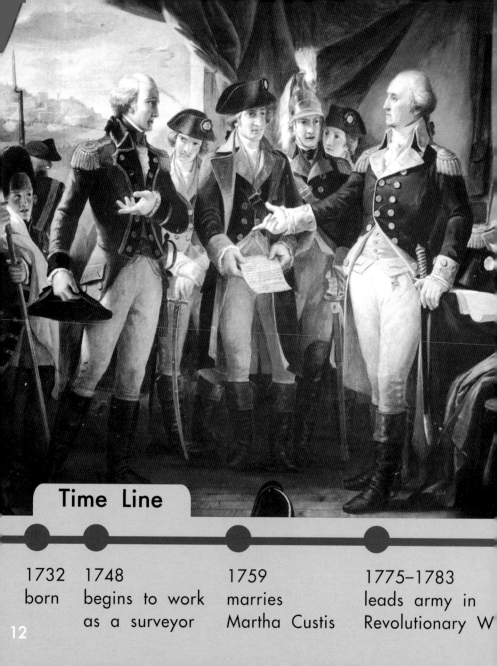

Time Line

1732
born

1748
begins to work
as a surveyor

1759
marries
Martha Custis

1775–1783
leads army in
Revolutionary W

The British lost the war in 1783. The colonists formed a new country called the United States of America. George returned to Mount Vernon after the war.

◄ George (right) spoke to the British about ending the war.

1783
returns to
Mount Vernon

Time Line

1732
born

1748
begins to work
as a surveyor

1759
marries
Martha Custis

1775–1783
leads army in
Revolutionary W

14

In 1789, Americans elected George as their first president. George was president of the United States until 1797.

◀ George (in black) was sworn in as president in New York.

1783
returns to
Mount Vernon

1789–1797
serves as
president

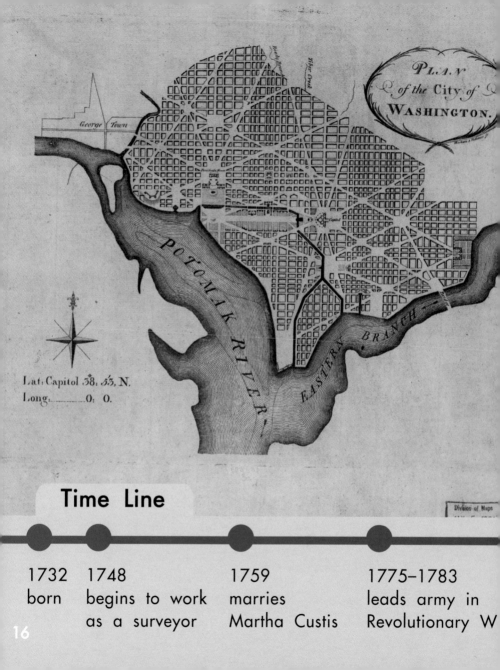

Plan of the City of Washington.

George Town

POTOMAK RIVER

EASTERN BRANCH

Lat: Capitol 38: 53, N.
Long: _____ 0: 0.

Time Line

1732	1748	1759	1775–1783
born	begins to work	marries	leads army in
	as a surveyor	Martha Custis	Revolutionary W

As president, George helped plan the capital city, Washington, D.C. He set up many parts of the U.S. government. He helped make the court system.

Plans for Washington, D.C., were drawn in 1792.

1783
returns to
Mount Vernon

1789–1797
serves as
president

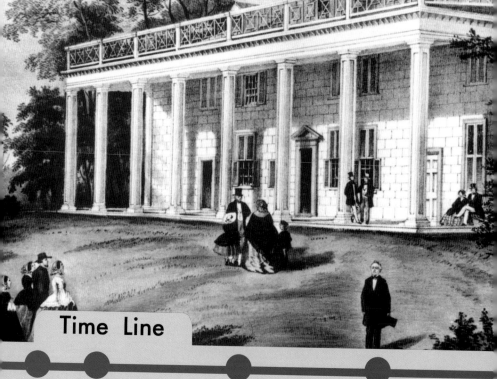

Time Line

1732
born

1748
begins to work
as a surveyor

1759
marries
Martha Custis

1775–1783
leads army in
Revolutionary W

Many Americans wanted
George to stay president
longer. But he said no.
He went home to Mount
Vernon again.

Mount Vernon, around 1850

1783
returns to
Mount Vernon

1789–1797
serves as
president

19

Time Line

1732
born

1748
begins to work
as a surveyor

1759
marries
Martha Custis

1775–1783
leads army in
Revolutionary W

20

George Washington died in 1799. Americans remember him as "The Father of His Country."

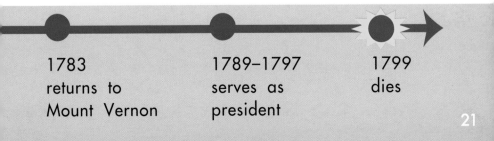

1783
returns to
Mount Vernon

1789–1797
serves as
president

1799
dies

Words to Know

capital—a city where a country's government is based; the U.S. capital is named after George Washington.

colonist—a person who lives in a colony; a colony is land ruled by another country.

elect—to choose someone as a leader by voting

government—the people who rule or govern a city, state, or country

plantation—a large farm where one main crop is grown

president—the elected leader of a country

Revolutionary War—the war in which the 13 American colonies won their independence from Great Britain; the Revolutionary War was fought from 1775 to 1783.

surveyor—a person who measures land and makes maps; George Washington made some of the first maps of Virginia.

Read More

Dubois, Muriel L. *The U.S. Presidency.* First Facts: Our Government. Mankato, Minn.: Capstone Press, 2004.

Gedacht, Daniel C. *George Washington: Leader of a New Nation.* The Library of American Lives and Times. New York: PowerKids Press, 2004.

Schaefer, Lola M. *George Washington.* Famous Americans. Mankato, Minn.: Pebble Books, 1999.

Internet Sites

Do you want to find out more about George Washington? Let FactHound, our fact-finding hound dog, do the research for you.

Here's how:

1) Visit *http://www.facthound.com*

2) Type in the **Book ID** number: **0736820825**

3) Click on **FETCH IT**.

FactHound will fetch Internet sites picked by our editors just for you!

Index/Word List

American, 11, 15, 19, 21
army, 11
born, 5
capital city, 17
children, 9
colonists, 11, 13
country, 13, 21
court system, 17
Custis, Martha, 9
died, 21
farm, 5
government, 17
Great Britain, 11
maps, 7
Mount Vernon, 9, 13, 19
plantation, 9
president, 15, 17, 19
remember, 21
Revolutionary War, 11
school, 5
surveyor, 7
United States of America, 13, 15
Virginia, 5, 7
war, 11, 13
Washington, D.C., 17

Word Count: 196
Early-Intervention Level: 18

Editorial Credits

Martha E. H. Rustad, editor; Heather Kindseth, cover designer and illustrator; Enoch Peterson, production designer; Linda Clavel, illustrator; Kelly Garvin, photo researcher; Karen Risch, product planning editor

Photo Credits

Corbis/Lee Snider, 4
Getty Images/Hulton Archive, cover, 1, 8, 12, 14, 18
Library of Congress, 6 (inset), 16
Stock Montage Inc., 6, 10, 20